SUGAR ART
Ideas

STENCILLING & AIRBRUSHING

SUGAR ART
Ideas

STENCILLING & AIRBRUSHING

LINDSAY JOHN BRADSHAW

Series Editor: ALISON LEACH

MEREHURST PRESS
LONDON

Published 1989 by Merehurst Press
Ferry House, 51-57 Lacy Road, Putney
London SW15 1PR

Co-published in Australia and New Zealand by Child & Associates, Unit C, 5 Skyline Place,
Frenchs Forest, 2086, Australia.

ISBN 1 85391 050 3

Managing Editor: Alison Leach
Designer: Richard Slater
Photographer: Graham Tann, assisted by Alister Thorpe, Lucy Baker
and Gary Taylor
Typeset by Vision Typesetting, Manchester
Colour separation by Scantrans Pte Limited, Singapore
Printed in Belgium by Proost International Book Production

ACKNOWLEDGEMENTS
The Publishers would like to thank the following for their help and advice:
Mr K. Vincent, Cotswold Cottage Graphics, Cotswold Cottage, Teddington,
Tewkesbury, Gloucestershire GL20 8JA
B. R. Mathews & Son, 12 Gipsy Hill, Upper Norwood, London SE19 1NN
Mrs E. A. Darnell, Morris & Ingram (London) Ltd, 156 Stanley Green Road, Poole,
Dorset BH15 3BE
Stencil Decor by Confectionery Design, 1 Thirlmere Avenue, Orrell Post, Wigan WN5
8PT
Wheatsheaf Graphics, 50 Grays Inn Road, London WC1X 8LT

Warning
Cocktail sticks and wired flowers must only be used for display purposes in sugarcraft. Great care
should always be taken to ensure there is no possibility of any particles being eaten accidentally.

CONTENTS

FOREWORD

It is always a pleasure to see a dedicated craftsman at work, because the genuine craftsman has that love for his subject which shines through everything he does and sets him apart from the rest of us. Lindsay John Bradshaw is such a craftsman, but he also possesses that rare ability to instil into both young and mature students the enthusiasm which makes them want to strive to emulate the high standards of their Instructor.

As an Assessor for the City and Guilds of London Institute in the 121 Certificate (Design and Decoration of Flour Confectionery), I have been closely associated with Lindsay John Bradshaw for a number of years now, and consider myself privileged indeed to have witnessed the results of his labours with the students at Salford College of Technology, where high standards of craftsmanship are a prerequisite.

His previous books on cake decoration have now been accepted as required reading by both students and working bakers, and I have no doubt that this new publication will take its place alongside them.

It is a beautifully written and illustrated guide to the somewhat 'lost' art of stencilling and airbrushing, set out in the easy to understand step-by-step format which has been the hallmark of the author.

After reading the book, I confidently predict an upsurge in interest in what has become perhaps a rather neglected, but nevertheless essential part of the true cake decorator's repertoire, and am certain it will be a welcome and valuable addition to the superb works Lindsay John Bradshaw has already written on the fascinating subject of cake decoration.

John Fann
Technical Services Manager
Peerless Food Products

INTRODUCTION

I am frequently asked by students and members of demonstration audiences about stencilling and airbrushing, two areas of sugarcraft that many people seem afraid to explore. Everything you need to know to launch you in these fascinating aspects of cake and confectionery decoration is included in this book.

As the series title suggests, this is primarily an ideas book but it also contains advice on choosing and using the right equipment and materials. Very little equipment is required for the stencilling process. As a cake decorator you will no doubt already have the few items you need to start immediately. Airbrushing does call for more specialized equipment, some of which can be expensive. However, the necessary information is provided to enable you to make the most practical investment to extend your range of sugarcraft equipment.

This book guides you through all the basic skills into intermediate projects and then to more advanced cake designs. Once you have mastered the techniques, you can produce original designs and effects by using imagination and creativity. The possibilities are endless and should give hours of pleasure to any cake decorator – and indeed their friends and customers who receive the spectacular creations.

There is no special secret to successful stencilling and airbrushing – just careful planning and preparation coupled with lots of imagination. Combine these qualities with the information in this book and you will soon gain confidence and derive considerable satisfaction from your efforts.

Lindsay John Bradshaw

BASIC EQUIPMENT

You will need these items when using stencils and airbrushes.

Oiled parchment paper available from art and craft shops or your local sugarcraft supplier may stock it

Thin card for making masks

Greaseproof paper for masking cakes when spraying

Masking tape for securing masks, templates and stencils

Cotton wool used for masking off, to create soft edges of colour

Cotton buds for cleaning airbrush or as a small moveable mask to create soft edges when spraying

Craft knife for cutting out hand-made stencils

Cutting board a clean, flat-surfaced small board to use when cutting out stencils

Cranked palette knife useful when stencilling in awkward areas

Scissors

Paintbrushes

Pencils

Small palette knife

STENCILLING

Stencilling is an easy, yet most elegant art form which is often used for the quick decoration of gâteaux and celebration cakes. When the sugarcraft boom started a few years ago, stencilling as a form of cake decoration was rather despised by many sugarcraft artists. With its bold and sometimes clumsy appearance through the conspicuous use of heavy 'ties', many designs did look mass-produced. Now, however, with the high quality of many pre-cut commercial stencils and the interest many cake decorators show in designing and cutting their own individual images, stencilling is undergoing a revival.

With a little time and effort taken over the choice of design, the preparation of the stencil and the introduction of intricate detail, it is quite difficult to detect that a stencil has been used to produce the multi-coloured images.

Stencilling can give beginners more confidence in decorating cakes. The fact that a precise image or inscription can be transferred in one simple application will spur many enthusiasts on to more adventurous creations. While still employing the basic stencilling technique, after a time you will be able to enhance the applied image to produce more advanced decorative work.

A definition of stencilling, as understood by the cake decorator, is the art of painting or applying coloured substances of any kind, through openings on a sheet of stout paper or metal, so that an impression is left on the surface underneath which may be royal icing, sugarpaste, chocolate or buttercream. All stencils are developments of this basic process, as the technique of application is the same whatever the design.

In addition to flat stencilling of food colouring or icing on to a prepared surface, stencilled pieces can also be formed on curved shapes to dry in a given form. The dried prefabricated pieces can then be made into flowers, water-lilies or other types of decoration.

Commercially available stencils made from stainless steel are very durable, easy to use and come in a range of designs from letters and numerals to animals and inscriptions. The full inscription stencils have the added advantage of register marks for easy repositioning.

Commercially available stencil packs contain designs in a range of different sizes, making them ideal for producing decorations for multi-tiered cakes. The stencils are precision-cut in oiled parchment paper and can be washed and used many times. Full instructions are included with numerous ideas on finishes and uses. Designs available are water-lilies, hearts, bells, flowers and easy to make butterflies.

For the creative sugarcraft artist hand-made stencils are probably the best choice. You can design and cut the stencil to your own exact requirements. Made from oiled parchment paper readily available from arts and crafts shops the stencils are cut out using a good sharp craft knife. They can be washed and re-used.

For quick one-off designs for topical or seasonal celebrations, cut a stencil from thin card. You can use this two or three times after rinsing, provided you place a weight on top while the stencil is drying to prevent it curling and warping. The stencil does however become distorted and loses its clear definition of shape, making it unsuitable for long term usage.

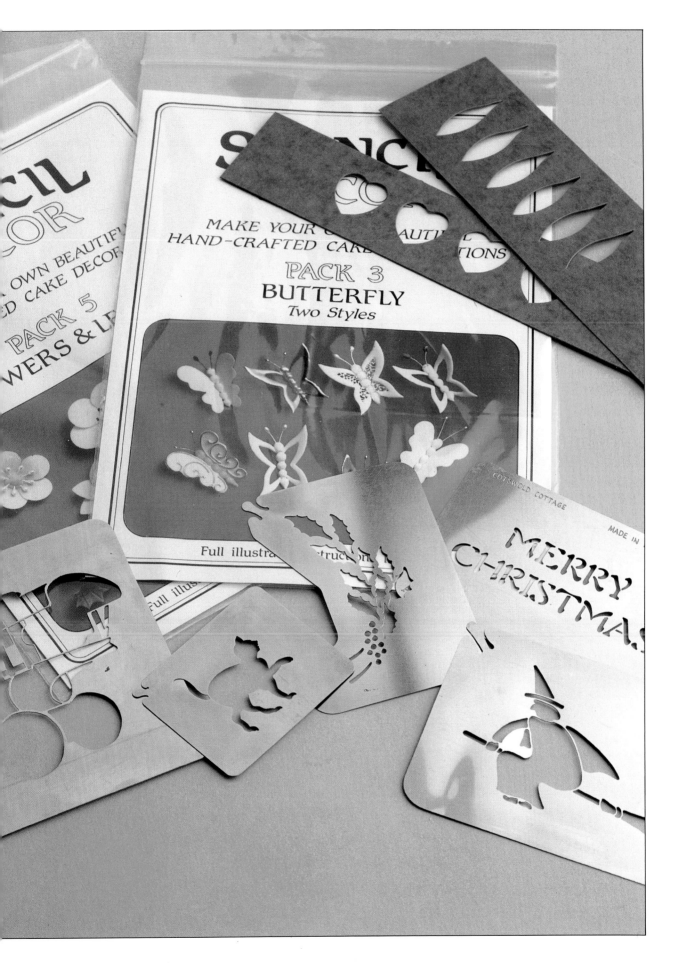

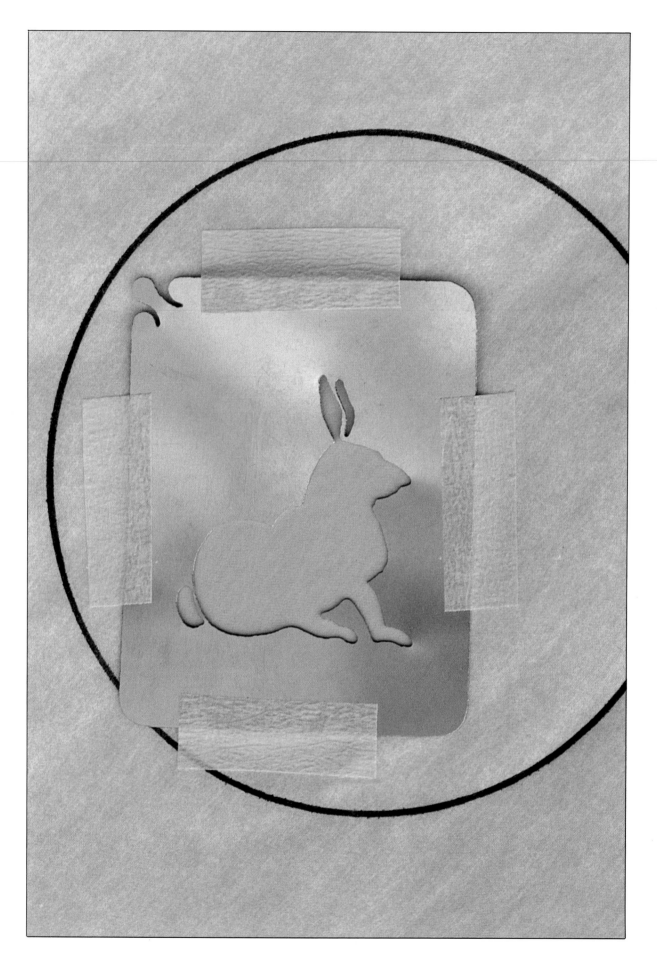

Making a stencil

The first drawing should be made regardless of ties and should be both accurate and quite natural. You must then decide where the ties are to be placed, the tie being the small strip of paper or card that links the parts of the cut-out design. Ties should only be used when absolutely necessary to keep the different parts of the stencil together and give it rigidity. They should be incorporated as cleverly as possible so that they seem to be part of the design. It is best to begin the design from as near a silhouette as possible, and add the ties later.

Cutting a stencil

Transfer the prepared stencil design on to parchment paper or thin card. If using parchment paper trace the design with a hard 2H pencil, then trace the outline on the reverse of the tracing paper with a softer HB pencil. Place the tracing on the parchment and outline with the 2H pencil. It can sometimes be difficult to see the image on the oiled parchment, and a better line definition will be reproduced in this way.

Place the stencil paper or card on your cutting board, and cut out using a sharp craft knife. This is a time-consuming process, but it is worthwhile making a neat job of the cutting as an oiled parchment stencil will last a long time if correctly cleaned and stored between use.

Take care when cutting lines that are very close together, apply a firm pressure on the craft knife to ensure good clean cuts. If you do make a mistake and cut out the wrong part, especially if nearing the completion of a very intricate stencil, you can repair it by pressing a piece of masking tape on the reverse of the damaged part, then turning the stencil over and re-cutting the area. This will not last as long as a perfectly cut stencil, but will save re-cutting a new one.

Using a stencil

Place the stencil on waxed paper, plastic wrap or a prepared cake surface. Ensure that the stencil cut-outs are in exactly the right position on the cake or waxed paper.

With your forefinger and thumb hold the stencil firmly on the surface. Do not allow the stencil or the waxed paper or cake to move during the stencilling operation.

Using a palette knife, spread a small amount of royal icing across the stencil to cover all the required cut-outs. Spread away from the end held by your forefinger and thumb across to the other end as shown. Spreading in the opposite direction would probably cause the stencil to buckle and lift.

Without disturbing the stencil (movement could distort the shapes) hold the waxed paper firmly (if stencilling on paper), then starting at the end opposite to the one being held, gently and carefully lift and peel off the stencil. If you have difficulty lifting the stencil, use the blade of a small knife to ease it. Use the same method of gently lifting and peeling off a stencil from a cake.

Prefabricated pieces for later assembly should be dried under a gentle heat such as a desk lamp as for run-out work. The stencilled sections will dry quickly and can then be removed from their waxed paper backing ready for use. For stencil work directly on to the cake top, allow the stencilled area to dry before starting further work on the cake.

Cleaning and maintenance of stencils

When stencils are used by cake decorators for sugar or food colour stencilling, they can be subjected to frequent washing in cold water. It is important to care for your stencils and store them correctly after use ready for the next time.

PARCHMENT TYPE After each use place the stencil in the sink under cold or lukewarm running water, and allow the water to flow over the stencil until no traces of icing or food colour remain. Remove the stencil from the sink and hold for a few seconds to allow most of the excess water to drain away. Then place the stencil flat on a clean tea towel laid on the work surface. Allow the stencil to dry fully for a few hours and then store flat ready for use.

If you intend to store a number of stencils together, interleave them with sheets of smooth paper or thin card to prevent the many ties and cut-out sections snagging together and damaging the stencils. On removing stencils which are packed flat together, take care not to drag them along each other; again damage to the stencil could occur.

METAL TYPE Wash as for parchment stencils, although hot water could be used here which will dissolve the icing or remove the food colour a little quicker than cold water would. Allow the excess water to drain off the stencil and then carefully dry with a soft cloth. Take care not to damage or snag the intricate parts of the stencil with the cloth when drying. Place the dry stencils back in their original packaging ready for the next use.

AIRBRUSHING

The basic cake decorators' kit from years ago, consisting of piping nozzles, flower nail, straight edge and side scraper, is a far cry from the equipment now available to the sugarcraft artist. The airbrush, in particular, has become very popular recently as an invaluable tool for achieving spectacular effects with edible colours.

An airbrush is a precision instrument. Before starting to use it, you must understand how it functions, how to maintain it and ensure maximum performance, and also be aware of its potential as another aid to creative sugarcraft.

The airbrush

The airbrush works on the principle of internal atomization. Compressed air (see below) flows through a nozzle which supplies food colouring. A partial vacuum at the front of the nozzle aperture makes the food colouring flow. The food colouring is then mixed with the compressed air and atomizes into tiny droplets to form a spray. The spray is controlled by a lever which regulates the ratio of air and food colouring.

The type of control, which alters the characteristics of the spray, identifies the different sorts of airbrushes available – single-action, double-action and independent double-action – making it a little easier for you to choose from the array of various brushes that will confront you when you decide to invest in one.

SINGLE-ACTION   This type of airbrush has only one control. When the push-button control is operated, the airflow draws the food colouring out to produce a spray. Because there is only one control, the ratio of food colouring to air cannot be altered. The only way to create different effects with this type of airbrush is to vary the distance between it and the icing surface or product being sprayed.

DOUBLE-ACTION   Variable food colouring flow is made possible by the double-action brushes. The control lever operates the air and the food colouring – when the lever is drawn back, the flow of both air and colouring increases. The ratio of food colouring to air cannot be varied even with this type of airbrush.

INDEPENDENT DOUBLE-ACTION   This type of airbrush is the most popular and inevitably more expensive. The ratio of food colouring to air is variable and is controlled easily by pressure exerted on the finger lever. Pressing the lever down controls the supply of air and a backward pulling movement allows the variable release of food colouring.

To explore the possibilities of this airbrush, the sugarcraft artist can spray a line as narrow as that produced by a fine piping nozzle and then continue to spray a large area of even colour in a single spray. If you wish to use airbrushing techniques to the full, this is the airbrush that you will most likely need to buy.

DESK CLIP   A simple and inexpensive desk clip can be purchased from your art shop or airbrush supplier. This will make the brush easier to use and there will be less spillage. The clip also holds the airbrush firmly while you pour in the food colouring ready for use, so it is a most worthwhile extra to your airbrushing kit.

Maintenance

Failure to maintain your airbrush properly may mean that your equipment turns out to be very expensive in the long term, due to what could be costly repair charges. It is essential that the airbrush is cleaned after every session of use, otherwise it will become clogged with food colouring and will be useless. Refer to the instruction manual provided with your airbrush, as each make of brush has to be dismantled in a slightly different way for cleaning.

To ensure true colours and good definition, the airbrush should be flushed through with water after removing any remaining colouring from the reservoir ready for a change of colour. Apart from regular cleaning of the food colouring channels, you should always check the needle in the nozzle to see that it is clean and straight. A sure sign of a bent needle is uneven, spattered colour; if this happens, replace the needle immediately with a new one. Never try to insert anything in the nozzle to clear it. Regular servicing by an expert is strongly recommended.

Air supplies

The sugarcraft artist who plans to do a lot of airbrushing would be wise to consider investing in a compressor. If you do not intend to use an airbrush very often, or you wish to experiment with its possibilities before outlaying a large sum of money, a simple aerosol propellant is the answer.

AEROSOL PROPELLANT   For the beginner this is usually the first choice. Experience can be gained by using this type of air supply which is quite

inexpensive. When you become more interested or practised, the extra cost of a more substantial air supply would be well justified.

The advantages of aerosol cans are their lightness, portability, quietness and the fact that no power supply is required to operate them. They are ideal for anyone who goes out demonstrating in halls where a power point may not be accessible, or whenever the least amount of equipment needs to be transported.

The main disadvantage is that as the air in the can is used up, the pressure falls considerably and will suddenly run out altogether, sometimes at a most inconvenient time such as when you are in the middle of a spray application on a cake top. A metered valve is available that helps to overcome this problem as it shows how much air is left in the can.

Without a valve it is more or less trial and error that tells you when to stop using the can. You can usually reckon that once the can is two-thirds used, you need to be ready for any problems occurring such as spattered colour, spitting and uneven pulses of pressure which can create an unwanted patchy effect. The cumulative cost of using a lot of aerosol cans can sometimes justify the purchase of a mini-compressor.

COMPRESSORS A range of compressors is available. The most basic one, ideal for the cake decorator, is a mini-compressor which operates one airbrush. Larger units for commercial use can run up to five airbrushes from one unit, enabling multi-coloured spraying techniques without the necessity to keep changing colours, as in a single airbrush. These are ideal for a busy cake decorating studio.

Mini-compressors consist of an electric motor driving a tiny piston or diaphragm. They are fairly inexpensive, costing about the same price as a good airbrush and are ideally suited to the cake decorator's requirements. The main disadvantage of a mini-compressor is that the air comes directly from the compressor and has a tendency to flow in short pulses which can sometimes affect the flow of food colouring, giving a patchy finish. Water filters are not normally fitted to mini-compressors and can lead to spots of water on your icing surface.

Most larger units usually incorporate a reservoir, which stores air at a constant pressure. Operation is either diaphragm or piston type, each having its own advantages. Because it is oil-free, the diaphragm compressor does not require an oil filter to be attached. Piston units are much sturdier and can be used to generate a higher pressure.

When you have gained confidence in lifting and laying masks, you can save yourself time by re-using masks that are already cut.

Lift the mask with the tip of a scalpel or craft knife so as not to damage the surface of your cake. Carefully peel back the mask, using only your finger tips. Remember to wash your hands thoroughly before positioning or removing a mask. Do not allow any colour, dirt or foreign bodies to get on to the back of the mask – any trace of dirt would be transferred on to the next cake surface and could be unremovable. Always place masks on a clean work surface or sheet of greaseproof paper.

PLASTIC MASKS You probably already have many of the artist's materials that will make ideal masks for various projects, such as circular and elliptical templates, stencils, plastic rulers and French curves.

Masking

Having spent some time acquainting yourself fully with your airbrush and its associated ancillary equipment, you will then need drawing equipment for planning your motifs or designs and masking materials to contain the flow of food colourings within specific areas.

Careful masking is just as important as the operation of the actual airbrush. Many cake decorators spend more time planning and cutting masks than actually spraying colour through them. Good results with even the simplest mask depend on planning and advance preparation.

First, study the figure or animal to be sprayed and note each colour to be used. Then make a simple plan or drawing on paper, working out how many masks will be required and in which order they should be used – numbering them will make the job easier at the spray application stage.

PAPER MASKS Paper can be used in several different ways to create useful masks. The straight edge of paper or thin card is obviously most useful when wishing to create straight sprayed edges. Equally the paper or card can be cut to any shape – round, oval, irregular, even in human and animal forms – enabling you to reproduce the most intricate detail or outline.

Torn paper with irregular edges makes ideal masks for creating soft edges for delicate, feminine and romantic themes; for wispy clouds and creative backgrounds to scenes or figures. To spray a still softer edge, hold the torn paper mask further back than normal and allow the air from the spray to get under the paper and vibrate it to give a really soft edge finish. Holding the paper near to the edge will keep it flatter and enable you to reproduce the exact outline of the torn edge.

COTTON WOOL MASKS Cotton wool, not surprisingly, will create excellent soft random edges. The cotton wool can be left to form irregular edges or can be made into more precise shapes for clouds, smoky effects and mottled backgrounds. Pulling cotton wool apart gently makes long uneven strands which, when laid on the cake surface and actually sprayed through, will create super sky, sunsets and modern coloured backgrounds. Use your imagination here to invent your own individual effects.

ACETATE A most durable material that lends itself ideally to airbrush work. The main advantage is that it is transparent and therefore allows you to see exactly what you are spraying. Any overspray of food colouring can quite easily be removed between sprays to retain the transparency of the material. Save pieces of acetate from cake ornament boxes or buy sheets in various sizes from your local arts and craft shop.

Erasers

Pencil erasers and kneadable putty rubbers can be useful both as creative aids and to get you out of trouble should you make mistakes. Very fine sandpaper is also good for removing traces of unwanted colour or small spots and splashes; use with only a light pressure, or white scratch marks will appear.

General advice

Remember that even though you can successfully freeze many decorated cakes if correctly packaged, some migration of sprayed colour will occur on defrosting the cake. This results in a blurred effect that is especially noticeable on what should have been crisp sharp edges of sprayed colour. Migrated colour will not be as obvious on sprayed colours that have been blended deliberately to create a particular effect. Try, therefore, to make, decorate and spray the cake a few days before freezing.

Initial colour backgrounds can be achieved by mixing the food colouring into the base icing or sugarpaste, or alternatively by spraying as a flat colour with an airbrush.

Leave sugarpaste-coated cakes to dry for about 12 hours in a dust-free place, ideally in the box in which the cake is going to be presented.

Sugarpaste-covered cakes are probably easier to spray than royal-iced cakes.

Using the airbrush

Much practice will of course be necessary to enable you to get the most from your airbrush. Practise basic lines, plain backgrounds and spraying round simple objects (masks) such as side scrapers and various cut-out shapes – do this on paper at first or a cake board coated with icing, rather than risk spoiling an iced cake. Once you have mastered these and also got the feel of your airbrush and understand its working principles, you can then move on to more adventurous and creative ideas.

Start work by connecting the airbrush to the hose and compressor or aerosol can. Don't be tempted to put any colour in the reservoir yet, just hold the airbrush, gently move the control lever and generally get to know the piece of equipment. Discover a comfortable spraying position where the hose is tucked neatly away from the spraying area. Then pour a small amount of food colouring into the reservoir of the airbrush. Switch on the air supply and you are ready to airbrush!

A few examples of what can be achieved by spraying are illustrated on pages 20 and 21.

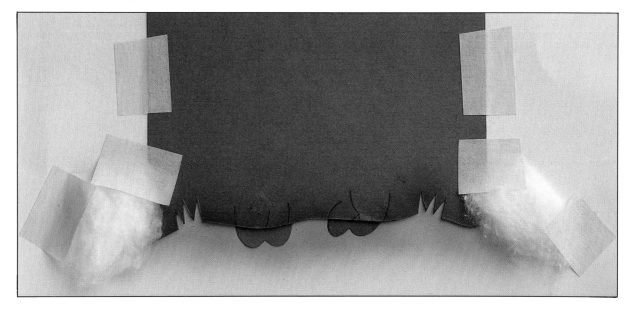

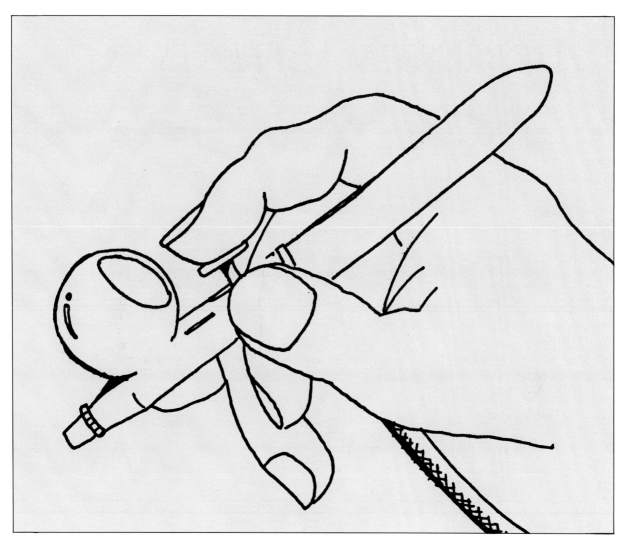

1 Hold the airbrush about 6–9mm ($\frac{1}{4}$–$\frac{3}{8}$in) away from the surface and spray a fine line, stopping the flow of food colouring before cutting off the air supply at the end of each line.

2 Now practise spraying thicker strokes by holding the airbrush further away from the surface. You will find that the further the airbrush is from the surface, the thicker the line will be.

3 After the above exercise, hold the airbrush still further away and move in even strokes to spray a large area of colour evenly.

4 Now repeat the previous exercises but this time make curved lines.

5 Having mastered straight and curved lines, try writing your name and then spraying tiny blossom flowers.

6 Using a mask of torn paper (tear the paper along a ruler), spray a line with an uneven edge.

7 Lift the paper mask slightly and spray against it to produce a soft-edged line.

8 Holding the paper loosely, spray into the torn edge of the paper allowing the air to vibrate the paper and produce a softer edge.

9 Holding the airbrush close to the surface, spray short sharp amounts of colour to produce dots. Move the airbrush further away from the surface to make larger dots. This technique is useful in a band of spots to appear like a ribbon around the sides of a cake. Dots are frequently used for highlights.

10 A simple paper mask such as a doyley can be used to practise spraying through paper. This would make a quick decorative finish for a cake top.

11 Spraying on flat dry sugarpaste through clean wire mesh will create an interesting grained effect, suitable, for example, for the table cloth on a teddy bear's picnic cake.

AIRBRUSHING EFFECTS

WATER-LILY DECORATIONS

These classic water-lily decorations find many uses as corner decorations on wedding cakes, or in that difficult-to-fill space in the centre of the tops of tiered cakes. See them used to good effect on the stencilled wedding cake on page 44. As a novelty feature they look particularly unusual on the frog pond cake (*see page 52*).

1 Prepare the petal shape of your choice as a stencil. Make the petals using the stencilling techniques (*see page 13*) with slightly softened royal icing.

The petals are made more interesting by drying them on curved formers, either concave or convex. Use centres from rolls of absorbent kitchen paper or specially purchased sugarcraft aids. Note the uppermost surface is the one that will be seen when used, so take this into consideration when designing and producing your water-lilies.

2 Prepare the bases for your water-lilies by making run-out discs in graduating sizes. Outline with a No1 nozzle and flood in with run-icing. Leave to dry. Decorate the edges of the discs with piped picot dot edging, scalloped lines or tiny piped shells.

Another attractive finish to the plaques, if the water-lilies are to be used as features, is to turn the disc upside down on an empty film container or clean empty paste colour jar. Pipe loops and leave to set. Turn the disc the right way up to reveal the attractive 'fence' edging. This technique can also be used on the disc when uppermost, but piped on the underside, which gives the appearance of the loops

supporting the plaque or disc.

Attach the prepared graduating-sized discs to each other with a little royal icing.

3 Position and attach the prepared stencilled petals with bulbs of royal icing. Concave petals will need supporting with small pieces of sponge until set. When set a

further group of convex petals can be attached. Finish the centres of the water-lilies by attaching a prepared piped icing bulb, or directly piping a bulb and inserting a few stamens while still soft. Piped spikes or dots, or sprinkled sugar can also be used to decorate the centre bulbs.

BUTTERFLIES

Butterflies have innumerable uses on decorated celebration cakes. They can be featured on wedding cakes on the corners, on cake side plaques and are especially attractive positioned near a spray of flowers on a cake top. You'll find the stencilled kind a lot easier and quicker to make than run-out ones.

1 Prepare a stencil from the butterfly shape of your choice. Place the stencil on the stencilling material and apply slightly softened royal icing using the technique described on page 13. Leave the wings to dry. Remember you will need left-hand and right-hand wings.

2 To assemble the butterflies, you will need to make a support former. Take a long oblong-shaped piece of thin card and fold to make a 'V'-shaped channel. Open or almost close in the card former depending upon what position

you want the butterflies' wings to be. Place a long, narrow, folded strip of waxed paper in the former. Carefully remove the dry wings and select the ones for use.

Using royal icing and a No2 nozzle, pipe a body on the fold of the waxed paper. Either pipe a bulb for the head and a long tapering body, or pipe five bulbs graduating in size from the head with the last one being pulled out to a point. While the body is still soft, insert a left and right wing into it. Also while the head and body are still soft, insert two tiny lengths of stamen for the antennae.

Various finishing touches may be added to the basic butterfly. Try overpiping the wings with a decorative line design using a No0 or No00 nozzle. The lines can then be painted with gold or silver food colouring. An airbrush can be used to spray tints of colour on to the wings and

body of the butterfly. For a really delicate effect, before assembling the butterflies, pipe filigree in the shape of each wing on to waxed paper. While the filigree is still soft, lay on a dry stencilled wing and gently secure in position. Leave the wings to dry and then assemble as before.

Painted butterflies

These butterflies really do look life-like and would be most attractive next to a spray of flowers. Stencil the wings as before (use the patterns provided to make your stencil), then paint the wing detail with edible food colourings. Borrow a book from your local library showing all the wing shapes and markings. Assemble the painted wings as before, inserting stamens which incidentally can also be painted in the actual real-life colour if wished.

HEARTS AND BELLS

Using prepared stencils of hearts and bells, you can quickly produce prefabricated shapes for cake decoration. The hearts and bells can be further decorated and then used to adorn your celebration cakes.

1 During the stencilling process the bells can be sprinkled with caster sugar to give them a frosty appearance. Arranged with some piped holly and berries, they make an ideal feature for your Christmas cakes.

The dry stencilled bell shapes can be painted with silver food colouring.

2 Stencilled hearts are left to dry and then edged with a piped coloured royal icing line using a No1 nozzle. These are useful for cake sides, corners of cakes and especially for the spaces that are sometimes formed in between run-out collars and piped borders.

Another way to decorate the hearts is to pipe filigree over the dry stencilled shape. The filigree can then be painted with gold or silver food colouring. Tiny dots piped around the edge of the hearts are yet another way to enhance them.

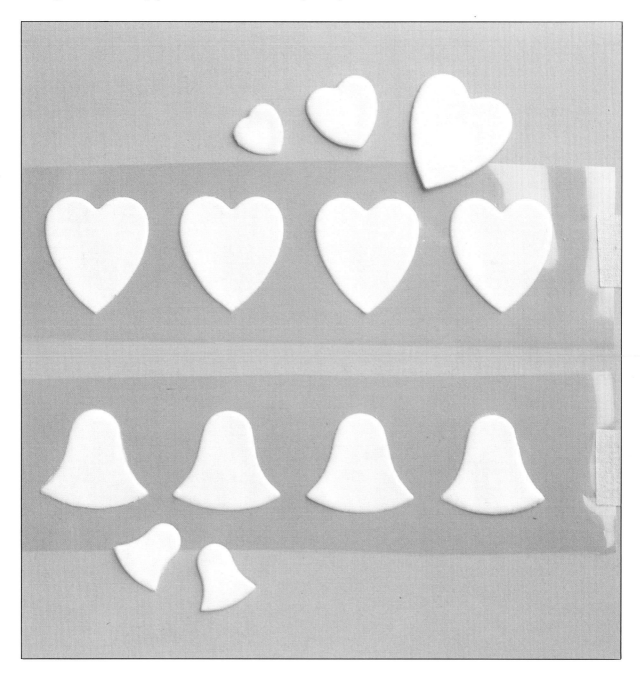

Flowers and leaves are traditionally associated with cake decoration. Stencilling provides another method of giving attractive floral touches to your decorated cakes.

1 Prepare a stencil using the required petal shape. As a guide, make your stencil contain the number of petals required for each flower plus one or two extra. In this way each time you stencil a 'run' of petals you will be sure to have sufficient plus a few spares in case any break. From then on, simply calculate the number of flowers you require for your cake.

Place the stencil on a waxed paper strip or plastic wrap, ensuring that the stencil cut-outs are within the waxed area. Apply slightly softened royal icing of the colour required using the stencilling technique described on page 13. Leave the stencilled petals to dry on a flat surface.

2 When the petals are completely dry, they may be given further detail by spraying either the pointed tip or the rounded end with a little tint of colour. You can use the same colour as the flower, spraying to make it very slightly darker, or use a contrasting colour.

3 To assemble the flowers you can use any of the three methods described below. First release the petals from the waxed paper, discarding any damaged ones. Place a piece of waxed paper on your work board and secure it with masking tape. Pipe a circle of royal icing (use freshly made icing that will retain its shape easily and hold the leaves in position) with a small bulb in the centre and insert the desired number of petals into it. You can insert the petals by the pointed tip or the rounded end depending on the type of flower you are creating.

Pipe another bulb and

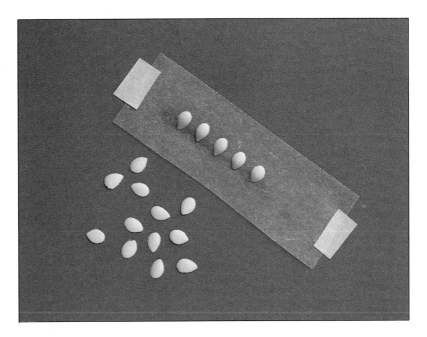

assemble the next flower. Continue until the required number of flowers have been made. Leave to dry.

To finish the flower, pipe a small bulb of coloured royal icing into the centre.

Another way of assembling the flower is to prepare small formers for each flower. Make these in plasticine and you can re-use them time and time again. Mould a ball of plasticine and press it on to your work board. Make a cup shape by making an indentation in the ball with your thumb or finger. Cut a small circle of waxed paper and press that into the former. Pipe a tiny bulb of royal icing in the centre of the paper circle and assemble the petals as described above. Finish with a bulb of icing in the centre.

When using this method of assembly, remove the dry flowers by inserting a cocktail stick (toothpick) between the waxed paper and the back of the flower, and gently releasing from the former, handling it very carefully.

The last method is based on the same principle as the plasticine former described above, but instead uses ready-made formers such as plastic sweet and chocolate inserts of the half-spherical shape.

4 You can be really creative by using different colours and textures to make a selection of delightful stencilled flowers. Note also the use of various centres. Pipe dots around the centre bulb, or pipe spikes around the centre bulb, inserting stamens into the soft centre bulb (remember flowers are no longer edible when they contain wire stamens) and even sprinkling the soft centre bulbs with coloured caster sugar or coloured non-pareils.

These easy-to-make plaques are ideal for the quick decoration of a celebration cake. Have some ready for those last-minute occasions! They also make nice gifts for cake decorators when they are packed in an attractive presentation box.

Roll out some coloured sugarpaste and cut out oval shapes with a food cutter. Leave the shapes to dry and then edge with a plain shell border, using royal icing with a No2 nozzle. Pipe the stems in green-coloured royal icing using a No1 nozzle. Then be creative! Arrange the prepared stencilled flowers of your choice to make an overall balanced design.

CHURCH SCENE

This method of airbrushing is executed with the aid of a simple card mask. The mask is cut out at each stage of the spraying process, with some cut-out sections being re-positioned at a later stage. This example of a Christmas church scene may be used on a royal-iced or sugarpaste-covered cake, or on a prepared piece of either material.

1 Prepare a template of the card mask from the pattern provided. Make the outlines clear and accurate as shown. Using a craft knife carefully cut out the tower and church wall. Position the mask on the cake top and secure lightly with a few pieces of masking tape, and apply a tint of orange colour. Remove the mask ready for the next stage. Note that the size of the mask is the same as the cake top or plaque, thus avoiding the need for any extra masking.

2 Cut out the next part of the mask which is the snow shape in the foreground. Re-position the mask on the cake top, aligning the previously cut-out area with the previously sprayed area. Secure with masking tape.
Repeat as for the previous steps, this time cutting out the

other two snow shapes on the left and at the front of the church.

3 Having completed spraying the church and snow shapes, cut a new mask of the church outline and top of the snow shapes. Position on the cake top accurately over the sprayed image. Hold the mask secure with masking tape and attach two small pieces of cotton wool as shown to create a soft edge to the extreme ends of the landscape scene. If cotton wool isn't used, a hard edge will appear where the airbrush has sprayed colour next to a straight edge such as the card mask or the edge of the masking tape. Spray blue colour, then a little violet colour to make a wintry sky. Also spray some soft-edged circles to make a background for the tree detail to be painted on.

4 The finished scene shows the painted church, trees and fence. The frosty effect is achieved by brushing the snow areas lightly with slightly softened royal icing. While still wet sprinkle a little caster (superfine) sugar over the area and then shake off the excess. The snow is formed by piping tiny dots of white royal icing and sprinkling them too with sugar. An extra mask was used here to create a more interesting foreground of light blue to represent snow.

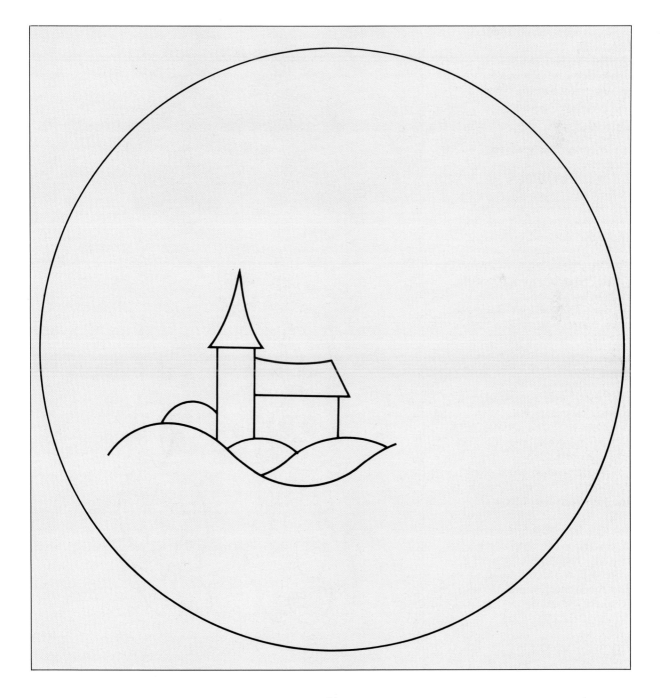

31

RABBIT FIGURES

The cake featured on page 56 shows this scene on a decorated celebration cake.

1 Cut out the stencil mask. Position on the cake top and secure with masking tape. Spray with orange colour.

Leave the mask in position and spray with brown colour. To give depth and modelling to the figure, spray on all the left-hand or all the right-hand sides. In the photograph the figure is sprayed on the left-hand side. The areas to be shaded (brown) will be determined by where you imagine you see the direction of light coming from.

2 Carefully remove the mask to reveal the sprayed figures.

Cut out a full mask or outline of each rabbit figure and position accurately over the sprayed images, ready to apply the sky and grass.

3 Cut a large mask to cover the figures and most of the picture area, with the tufty grass outline cut out along the base. Reserve the lower half of the mask for later use. Carefully position over the rabbit masks and secure with masking tape. Note when preparing such a mask that requires accurate re-positioning, make some sort of register marks such as the feet and leg outlines.

Use the cotton wool edge method to mask off the edge of the grass outline; this will soften the edge and not leave a straight line of sprayed colour. Spray the grass with green colour, then highlight with a little yellow, then orange to add more interest and detail. Remove the mask.

4 Using the reserved lower half of the previously cut mask, position it at the base of the still-in-position rabbit masks and previously sprayed green colour. Edge off once again with cotton wool and then apply blue colour with the

airbrush. Remove the mask, cotton wool and rabbit masks to reveal the complete sprayed areas.

Complete the scene by painting in the remaining detail with edible food colourings and fine paint brushes.

HOLLY PLAQUE

To avoid applying lettering directly to your cake top which can sometimes be a problem, make a plaque as shown so that you can practise and get the lettering just right to place on your beautifully decorated cake!

1 Make a run-out disc in royal icing and use a commercial stencil to apply a festive or other inscription. Leave to dry. To complete the plaque, pipe a small plain shell border around the edge using white royal icing and a No2 nozzle.

Pipe the holly leaves in green-coloured icing using a No1 nozzle; then with a paintbrush neatly pull out spikes to make the characteristic holly outline. Pipe a few red berries and then with white royal icing, pipe an icicle formation beneath the inscription.

While still soft, sprinkle with caster (superfine) sugar to give a frosty effect, shaking off any excess sugar.

34

LONG SNOWMAN AND SNOWFLAKES

Two very simple stencils are used to create the novel decorations for this cake – a good introduction to stencilling and airbrushing techniques.

1 Cut out the cake shape from an oblong cake. Cover the cake in the usual way with pink-coloured sugarpaste and leave to dry for a few hours.

2 Cut out the simple snowman shape using a template of the pattern provided.

Place the stencil on the prepared cake and apply white royal icing (*see page 13*). Remove the stencil and immediately sprinkle the icing with caster (superfine) sugar. Shake off any excess to reveal a frosty snowman shape.

35

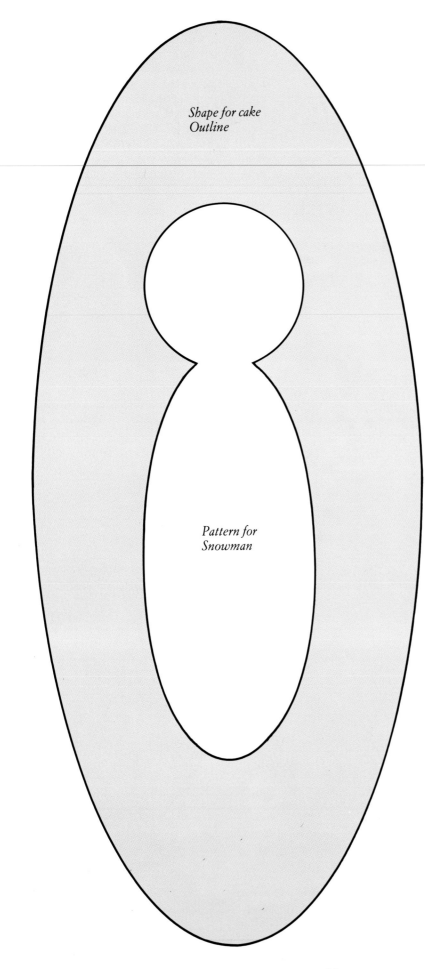

Shape for cake
Outline

Pattern for
Snowman

3 Cover a long oval-shaped cake board with white sugarpaste and decorate the edge using crimpers. Leave the sugarpaste to dry for a while. Make a snowflake stencil with a template of the pattern provided. Hold the snowflake stencil on to the cake board and spray with blue colour. Make a random pattern of snowflakes all over the board. Attach the cake securing with a little royal icing.

4 Decorate the bottom edge of the cake with a small shell border piped in white royal icing. Attach a pink ribbon and bow to the cake side and pipe a scallop line in pink-coloured royal icing, using a No1 nozzle, around the top edge of the cake. Decorate the snowman with various colours of royal icing to make his facial features, hat, scarf and buttons.

Pattern for Snowflake

TEDDY CAKE

Another attractive cake, featuring a simple stencil this time with the use of ties to make a more detailed and interesting figure. Again caster (superfine) sugar is used to good effect to create a texture on the body of the teddy.

1 Cover an oblong cake with coloured sugarpaste; the colour used on the cake in the photograph is paprika paste colour. Make a fancy edge around the top of the cake by using crimpers to create a decorative pattern.

2 Cut out a stencil using a template of the pattern provided.
   Place the stencil on the cake top, securing with masking tape. Apply paprika-coloured

royal icing, using the stencilling technique (*see page 13*). Leave the stencil in position and while the icing is still soft, sprinkle it with paprika-coloured caster (superfine) sugar. Carefully shake of any excess sugar and then remove the stencil to reveal the textured teddy shape. The stencil may be removed from the cake as for the Long Snowman cake (*see page 35*), but as this stencil has ties, a more accurate finish is achieved by leaving it in position when applying the sugar.

3 The textured teddy shape is then ready for further decoration. Pipe a small shell border around the cake base with paprika-coloured royal icing and a No44 nozzle.

4 Complete the teddy bear by piping in the various facial features with coloured royal icing. The stitching on the body and the markings for the paws are piped using a No2 nozzle and black-coloured royal icing. Make the bow tie by rolling out some yellow-coloured marzipan and pressing into it some tiny balls of blue marzipan, then re-roll the marzipan to make it smooth with a spotted pattern, cut out two triangular shapes and attach with a ball of marzipan using a little egg white.

5 A hand-made stencil is used to apply the name of your choice directly on to the cake top. Position a stencilled flower and a couple of gold leaves at each corner of the cake. A pretty coloured ribbon and bow around the cake side add the finishing touches.

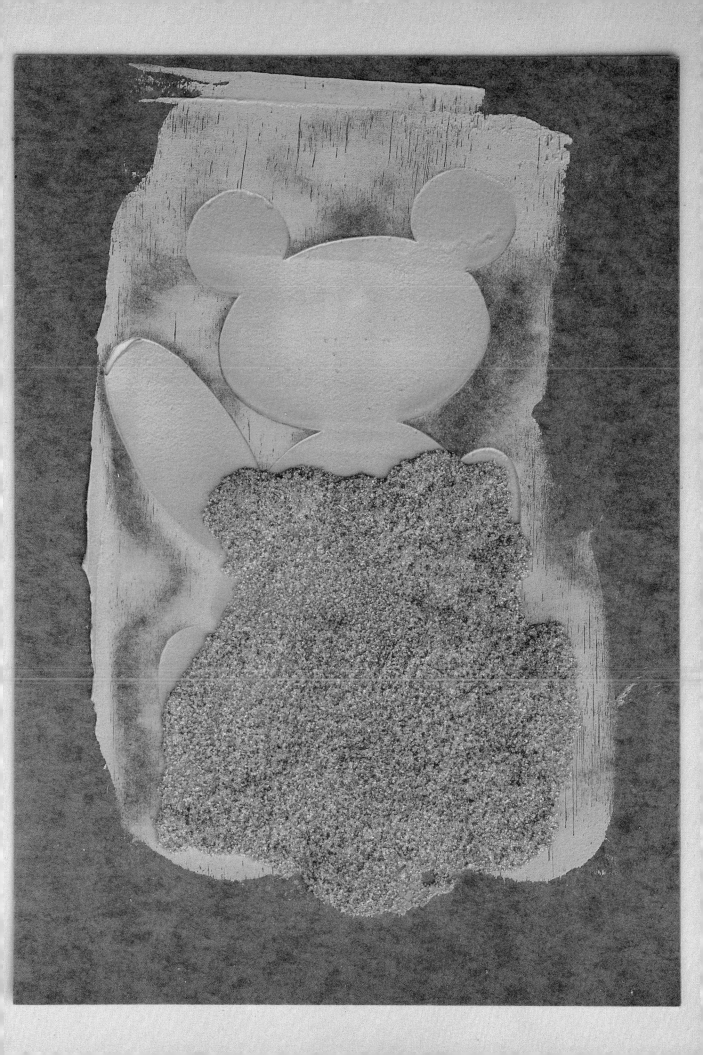

SPACE AGE CAKE

This birthday cake would delight any youngster. It is quick to make once the stencil has been cut – remember you can use the design stencil over and over again.

1 Cover a large round chocolate cake with melted plain chocolate. The cake could be layered with chocolate buttercream. To coat the cake, place it on a wire rack with a sheet of greaseproof paper beneath, pour the melted chocolate over and let the excess drain on to the paper. Give the wire rack a gentle tap to assist the flow. Leave to set.

2 Place the prepared stencil on the cake top and apply the various prepared colours of royal icing. The lettering is in blue while the flames at the rear of the rocket are a partly mixed combination of yellow-, red- and orange-coloured icing. The remaining parts are all in white.

When the stencil icing is dry, paint the rocket and spaceperson's helmet with silver food colouring. The face is painted with pink colouring.

3 To complete the cake, pipe the words 'Have a' and 'Birthday' in bright orange-coloured icing using a No2 nozzle. Pipe the base border in piping (thickened) chocolate using a No44 nozzle.

EASTER GATEAU

A very simple but tastefully effective way to decorate your Easter table centrepiece. The decorated sugarpaste sections can be made well in advance and stored ready for use. All the decoration is made off the cake and then added when exactly right.

1 Sandwich and layer your sponge in the usual way and coat with buttercream of the flavour and colour of your choice. Cream or lemon colour, as used in the photograph, looks lovely for Easter. Mask the sides with roasted almond nibs and place the cake on a silver cake board.

2 Roll out some sugarpaste of the same or a contrasting colour to that of the buttercream used to coat the cake. Measure the diameter of your gâteau and cut out a circle of sugarpaste of the same diameter as the coated cake. Using a small round cutter remove and retain a circle of paste from the centre of the large circle. With a sharp knife and a ruler cut the circle into twelve equal sections as shown. Leave the pieces to dry.

3 The sugarpaste sections are each stencilled with an Easter motif. A commercial metal stencil was used here to apply the duck motif. Use egg-yellow-coloured icing for the body and orange-coloured for the beak and feet.

Using the same principle described above, celebration cakes for many varied occasions can be decorated with appropriate themes for Hallowe'en, Christmas, birthday, Mother's Day and so on!

STENCILLED WEDDING CAKE

This stunning cream-coloured wedding cake really makes use of the stencilling techniques already described in this book – there are even stencilled collars.

1 First make the stencilled collars. Cut a stencil incorporating three different sizes of template from the patterns provided (*see page 46*) Make the stencil from a card about 3-mm (⅛-in) thick. This will give added stability to the pieces when stencilled and dried. Stencil sufficient shapes for your multi-tiered cake. You will need sixteen shapes for each cake, but it is wise to make a few extra in case any are damaged. Leave the shapes to dry.

When the shapes are fully dried, pipe delicate filigree work over each one using a No1 or No0 nozzle and cream-coloured royal icing.

2 Make a template to divide the cake into four equal sections. Place on the cake top. Then make strips of card to pipe the side design against. To measure the width of these side pieces, it is a good idea to arrange your prepared stencilled collar sections in groups of four on a circle drawn on paper of the same diameter as the coated cake; the spaces in between will determine the width of the panels. Pipe vertical lines down the cake side, using a No2 nozzle. Tilt the cake to make piping easier.

3 The large spaces between the narrow panels on the cake side are piped with four dropped loops. Mark the top template with dots to make piping more accurate. Make a template from the drawings provided and position on the cake board. Pipe line-work as shown. A card circle with a section removed is used as a template to pipe link line-work on the board.

4 Make a series of water-lilies (*see page 22*) in cream-coloured royal icing in three graduating sizes to be used on the corners of the cake in between the collar sections.

5 The finished wedding cake is assembled with cream-coloured cake pillars and an attractive arrangement of colour co-ordinated silk flowers. The side panels on the cakes are decorated with various stencilled off-pieces with butterflies, hearts and bells painted with gold food colouring to complement the overall effect. In the space between the cake pillars an extra special water-lily is featured with piped petals painted with gold food colouring.

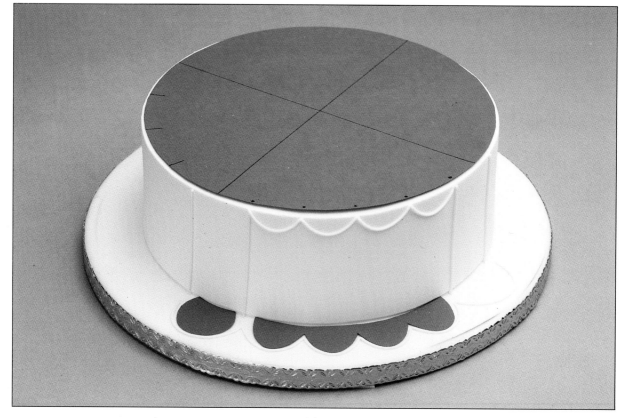

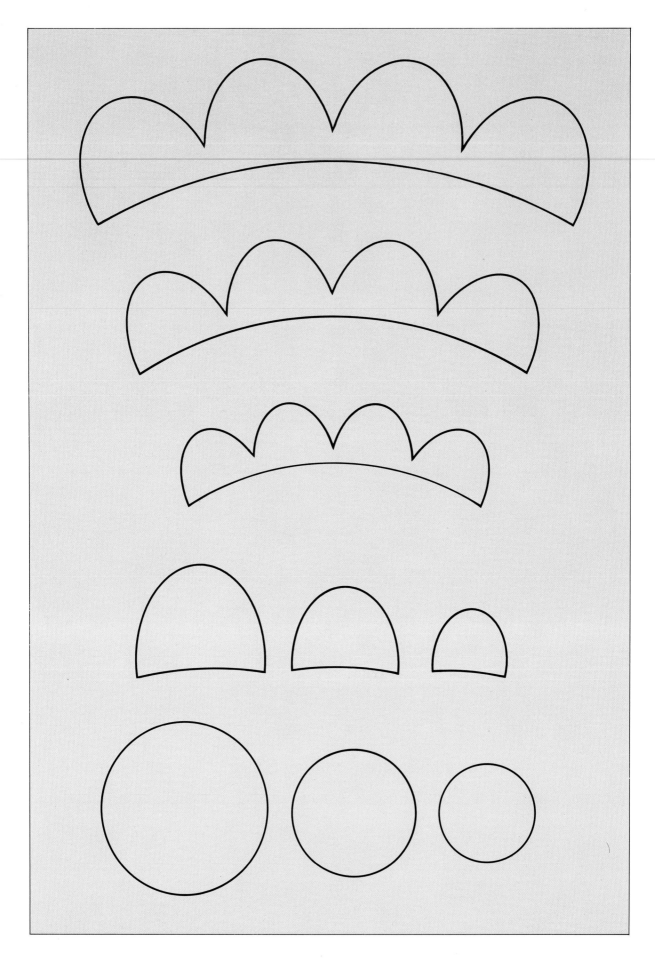

BUZZY BEE CAKE

Bake two sponge cakes in pudding basins, one large and one small. Sandwich the cakes with jam and buttercream. Alternatively a rich fruit cake mixture could be used.

1 Turn the cakes upside down, brush with boiled apricot jam and cover them with yellow-coloured marzipan. On the larger cake, indent the 'honey pot' texture on the side of the cake using the round handle of a wooden spoon held horizontally to the cake side.

2 For the lid of the honey pot, leave the smaller cake plain without any indentations. Make a rim for the lid by rolling out a large rope or roll of marzipan. Attach the rim to the lid with a little egg white. Make a ball of marzipan and attach to the top of the lid.

3 Place the cake on a turntable to make spraying easier and more consistent. Using the airbrush, spray the cakes with orange colour first, spraying from a distance to give a good overall covering. Then spray into the grooves or indentations on the cake side with dark brown colour, holding the airbrush quite close to the cake to make narrow lines of colour.

4 Pipe some bulbs and tear shapes of royal icing for the dribbles of honey. Leave to dry. Spray the shapes first with yellow and then orange to create a honey-coloured appearance. Leave a small section of white when spraying to create a highlight and make a 'glossy' effect.

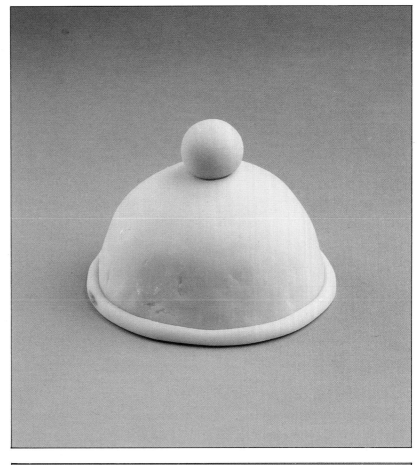

5 Make the honey pot label. Cut out an oval shape of brown marzipan. Stencil the border and 'honey' detail on the prepared shape, using yellow- and orange-coloured icing. Mask off the areas individually if it makes application easier. When dry, paint the border with gold food colouring.

6 Using a metal flower petal cutter, cut out two wings for each bee from white flower paste. Leave to dry. Spray the wing edges with a light tint of blue and then paint on very fine veining with a No0 paintbrush and light grey food colouring made by mixing a little black paste colouring with white powder colouring preparation.

7 Make the buzzy bees by rolling out two rolls of marzipan, one coloured black and one egg-yellow. Cut both rolls into sections.

Re-assemble the sections to form rolls of alternating colours. Gently squeeze and shape the rolls to form an oval body shape. Insert two prepared dry wings into the soft body. Support the wings with a little sponge if necessary until set.

8 Make the head, tail and tiny nose from black-coloured marzipan. Indent the eyes in the head using a ball modelling tool. Attach all the parts to the bee with egg white, then pipe in the eyes with royal icing, overpiping with brown icing.

9 Prepare the cake board by covering with green-coloured marzipan and decorating the edge with crimpers. When the honey pot is in position, the board can be sprayed with green food colouring to make a more interesting presentation. Attach the drips of honey, the bees and the label with a little royal icing. Finish the board edge with velvet ribbon or gold band.

ARTIST'S PALETTE

A birthday celebration cake, just right for the budding artist or serious enthusiast! The palette is easily cut from a sheet of sponge cake. The top and sides are then covered with sugarpaste.

1 Make the wood-grained top by only partly mixing paste colours of orange, yellow and brown, and rolling out to give a streaky finish. Pipe blobs of brightly coloured royal icing for the paints. Model the artist from marzipan with a few marzipan paint brushes.

2 The white sugarpaste oblong is prepared and dried off the cake and the inscription applied with a hand-made stencil of the lettering style you choose.

3 Using the drawing provided, cut out your lettering stencil as shown.

FROG POND CAKE

This amusing little novelty cake uses both stencilling and airbrushing in the decorative techniques.

1 Make a template from the drawing provided (*see page 64*) and place this on your prepared sponge or rich fruit cake. Cut out the cake in the kidney shape. Any crumbs and trimmings can be used to make various sweets and treats, so don't throw them away! Cover the cake and cake board in blue-coloured marbled sugarpaste.

To make the marbled sugarpaste, mix some dark blue- and light blue-coloured pieces of sugarpaste into white sugarpaste, adding a few streaks of blue paste colouring applied with a cocktail stick (toothpick). Partly mix the mass and then roll out as usual to create the marbled effect. Leave the surface to dry for a few hours.

2 When dry, pipe lines of moss green-coloured royal icing, using a No2 nozzle, from the base upwards. Using the airbrush, apply shades of green, yellow and then orange food colouring to colour the grass edging.

3 Prepare the lily pads from the patterns provided. Using the stencilling technique (*see page 13*), apply moss green-coloured royal icing to the cake top through the lily pad stencils. Remove the stencils and leave the shapes to dry.

When dry, use edible paint pens to outline the lily pads and paint on the veining.

4 To make the frogs, mix some green-coloured modelling marzipan, using green with a little egg-yellow and a spot of tangerine food colouring. For the arms and legs, model a long carrot shape from a ball of marzipan. Make an indent near the end for the hand or foot and then make three cuts with a small knife. Fan out the cuts to make fingers or toes. For the body, model a pear shape from a large ball of marzipan. For the head, model a flat pear shape from a ball of marzipan. Use a ball modelling tool to make indentations for the eyes and then use a small knife to make a slit for the mouth. Thin out and shape the edge of the mouth with your finger and thumb.

5 Assemble the frog, using egg white to join the parts together. Pipe the eyes with white royal icing and a No2 nozzle, overpiped in brown with a No1 nozzle. A red tongue completes the model. Assemble the frogs in various positions and also attach the heads at different angles to make the overall effect more lively!

6 Make the pink water-lillies using the method described on page 22, including a few flat dried petals. Assemble each water-lily by fixing six flat petals together with a little royal icing. Then attach six curved petals over the joins of the flat petals. Spray the finished water-lily with bright pink food colouring and then insert a centre of pink-coloured marzipan that has been pushed through a tea strainer, sieve or clay gun. Colour the tips of the marzipan stamens with pink petal dust or food colouring.

Attach the prepared water-lilies and the frogs to the cake top with royal icing.

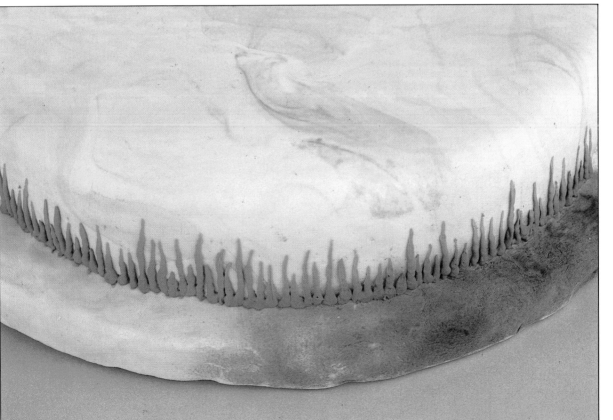

RABBIT AND PINK HEARTS CAKE

This interesting cake design could be used for a birthday, engagement or Valentine celebration. Stencilling and airbrushing techniques are used extensively on this colourful, yet tastefully decorated creation. The side design is stencilled directly on to the cake. Instructions for spraying the rabbits and background are given on page 32.

1 Make four run-out top collars and four base collars using the templates made from the patterns provided; also make the overlay sections. When dry, stencil the overlay sections with heart shapes using pink-coloured royal icing.

2 For the side decoration, the hearts can be applied in royal icing or sprayed with food colouring according to choice. If using royal icing, prepare a stencil with four heart shapes. Position the stencil on the cake side and secure with masking tape. Using the stencilling technique (*see page 13*), apply pale pink-coloured royal icing. Remove the stencil to reveal the stencilled shapes.

3 The heart shapes can be left as they are or outlined with a fine brighter pink line using a No1 nozzle. Alternatively, spray tints of pink and then a little red and brown colouring to give a roundness to the heart shapes.

4 After applying the sprayed and painted rabbits to the cake top, the sides are piped with drop loop linework. When the run-out collar sections are in position, pipe linework around them on the cake top and the board.

An effective use for stencilled flowers and leaves is to position them at the corners of the cake as shown.

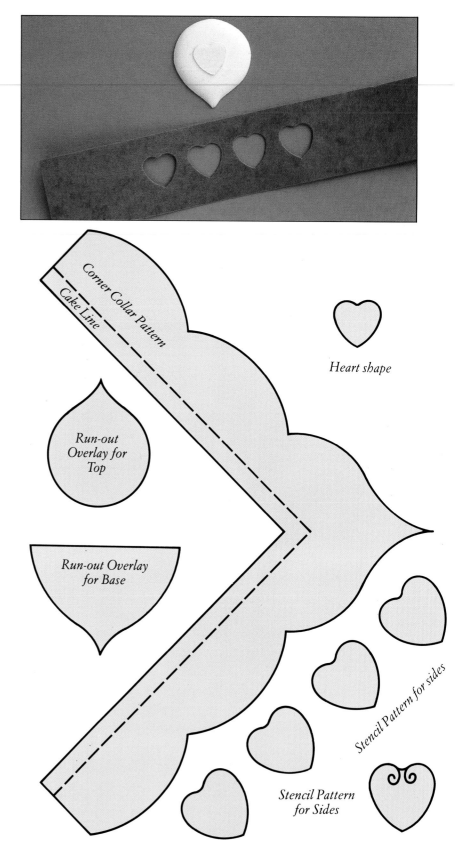

Corner Collar Pattern

Cake Line

Heart shape

Run-out Overlay for Top

Run-out Overlay for Base

Stencil Pattern for sides

Stencil Pattern for Sides

BIRDS AND GOLD RING CAKE

1 Cover a large round cake with white sugarpaste in the usual way and leave to dry for a few hours.

Make a card mask of a heart shape of the appropriate size, position at an angle on the cake top and place a light weight on top to prevent any movement. Apply pink food colouring using an airbrush and spraying reasonably close to the edge of the heart shape to achieve a faded effect. Remove the mask.

2 Change the colour in the airbrush to violet and spray tiny flower shapes by holding the airbrush quite close to the cake surface. Before using this design on a real cake, it is recommended that you practise by spraying a few flower shapes on a piece of card. Pipe a tiny bulb of royal icing in the centre of each flower and leave to dry. When dry, carefully paint the flower centre with silver food colouring.

3 To make the birds, first prepare the wings. Roll out some flower paste thinly and cut it as for a Garrett frill. The centre circle should, however, be made with a smaller cutter than would be used for a Garrett frill. Cut the prepared shape into four sections.

4 Then take each section and frill the edge by rolling with a cocktail stick (toothpick). Before the paste starts to dry, gather and pinch the shape to form a fan shape, place on your work board and leave to dry completely. Make two wings and a tail for each bird.

EGG-SHAPED DAFFODIL CAKE

Why not make this unusual cake for your table centrepiece at Easter? The cake is baked in a round cake tin (pan) and then cut to an egg shape with a template.

1 Layer the cake and then coat with chocolate buttercream. Mask the sides with chocolate vermicelli and pipe a shell border with piping (thickened) chocolate around the top and base. Present the cake on a gold board to give a rich appearance. Decorate the board with orange-coloured linework and yellow-coloured filigree.

2 To decorate the run-out plaque, first make a greaseproof paper mask to cover the run-out and do not allow any sprayed particles of colour to settle on it. Cut a space in the mask and position your stencil – in this instance a commercial stainless steel stencil is used. Secure the mask to the stencil with a little masking tape.

3 The colours and details for the rabbit plaque are built up gradually. Apply an even tint of orange colour to the rabbit. Next apply a dark shade of brown. In the photograph

all the shaded brown areas appear in the bottom left of each form of the animal. The position of the shaded areas will obviously depend on where you imagine the direction of light to be.

Remove the mask and rabbit stencil. Spray a little green colouring at the base of the rabbit to simulate grass, so that the rabbit does not appear to be floating in mid-air! Blue colouring can then be applied for the sky. Finish the plaque by painting in the features of the rabbit and also some groups of daffodils.

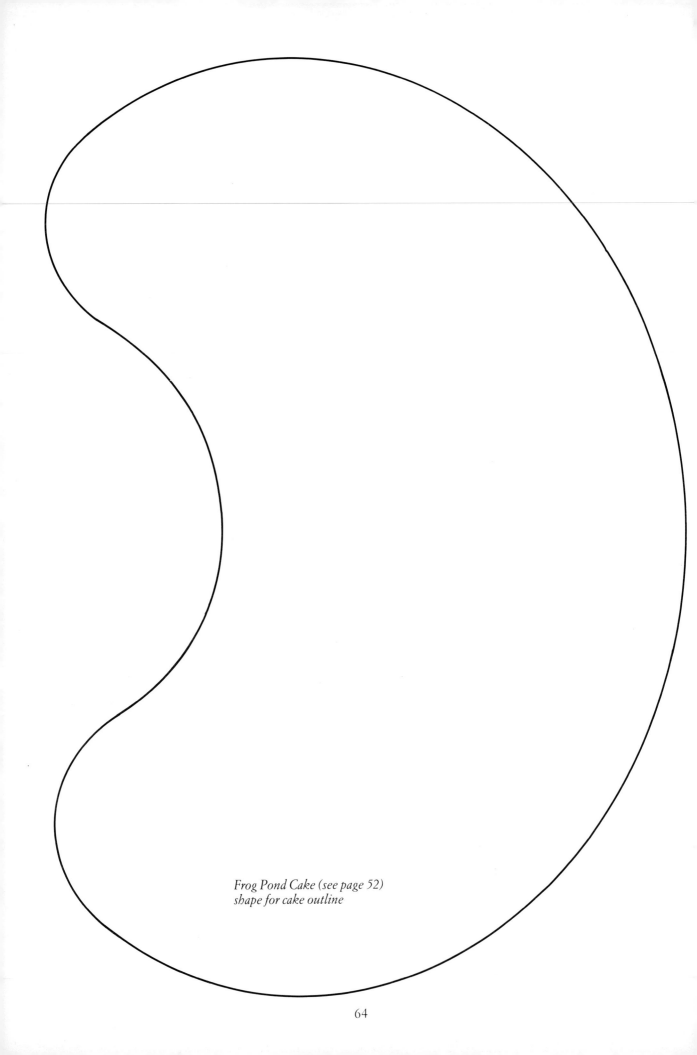

Frog Pond Cake (see page 52)
shape for cake outline